14th Anniversary Edition

THE LOST ART OF SCRATCH COOKING

*Recipes From The Kitchen
Of
Natha Adkins Parker*

By
Curtis Parker

Published by:
Curtis Parker
5050 Laguna Blvd., Suite 112-427
Elk Grove, CA 95758
Email: tocookgood@aol.com

© 1997 by Curtis Parker
All rights reserved. No part of this book may be reproduced, stored in a retrieval system, or transmitted in any form or by any means, electronic, mechanical, photocopying, recording or otherwise, without the prior permission of Curtis Parker.
First Printing in 1997

14th Anniversary Edition, July 2011
Reprinted by permission of the author.

New Edition Graphic Design – Roulston Love Frye
(www.roulstonlovefrye.com)

14th Anniversary Edition Project Management
Jabez Enterprise Group (JEGroup)
www.jabezenterprisegroup.com

Front Cover
Photography - Robert Fong
Original Design Graphics - Diana's Graphic Designs

Back Cover
Photography - Bill Jones
Original Design Graphics - Diana's Graphic Designs

Library Of Congress Cataloging-in Publication Data
Parker, Curtis
The Lost Art of Scratch Cooking/Curtis Parker
ISBN 13-9780615518053
CIP 97-94703

Printed in United States of America

To My Mother:
NATHA LEE PARKER

N - NICE: all the nice things you do for others.

A - ALWAYS: always ready for whatever or whoever you are needed for.

T - TIRELESS: never too tired to go that extra step.

H - HAVING: having time always for children, friends and family.

A - ANSWER: able to supply an answer to some of life's problems.

L - LOVING: loving always for your family, no matter what the need or distance.

E - EXCEPTIONAL: strength and courage to go that extra step.

E - ENDURANCE: able to stand the test in good times and in bad times.

PARKER: for all the wonderful children you brought into this world!

With Love
Written by Dorothy Parker Skanes (Natha's fourth child and second daughter)

Table of Contents

ACKNOWLEDGMENTS	VI
ABOUT THE AUTHOR	VII
ABOUT THE COOK	VIII
BREADS & ROLLS	11
DESSERTS	25
EGG DISHES	45
MEATS & MAIN DISHES	51
SALADS	65
SAUCES	75
SIDE DISHES	83
SPECIALTY ITEMS	91
VEGETABLES	103
BONUS RECIPE:	
PEACH COBBLER	107
MORE OF NATHA'S TIPS	109
INDEX	113

Acknowledgments

To my beautiful wife, Pamela who provided inspiration and editing.

To my children Monica and Curtis Jerome who provided layout ideas and continuous love and support

About the Author

Curtis Parker is the ninth child and fifth son of J P Parker and Natha Adkins Parker. He resides in Elk Grove, California with his wife Pamela. They have two children and three grandchildren.

Curtis is a member of Saint Paul Missionary Baptist Church of Sacramento, California. He is very active in his church ministries serving as one of the Associate Ministers, Member of the Male Chorus, Teacher in the New Membership Department and member of the Combined Choir.

Other community activities include serving as bass singer and Business Manager of the Internationally Acclaimed "Voices of Faith", a choral ensemble under the leadership of Curtis' mother-in-law, Dr. Precious Craft. This group has as its primary focus the preservation of the Negro Spiritual as an art form and educational experience. They have traveled extensively throughout the United States and took their first European Tour in 1996.

In his professional life, Curtis spent twenty (20) years working for the Sacramento Employment and Training Agency (SETA), this served as the workforce development administration for the county of Sacramento. In his position as Operations Division Chief, Curtis was responsible for managing economic development, marketing dislocated workers and Military Base Closure programs. Later he served as Vice President of Operation for ROC Diamond Record where he was responsible for developing business relationships and marketing the company's gospel division. Curtis was called into service with the American Red Cross and has served with the Sacramento Sierra Chapter, The Pacific Service Area Office, Partnership Development Manager for The State Of California and most recently as a Program Manager for The National American Red Cross Corporate Diversity Department.

Last but certainly not least, Curtis is an excellent cook. Under the watchful eye of his mother, he has managed to master the LOST ART OF SCRATCH COOKING.

About the Cook

Natha Adkins Parker was born on February 13, 1923 in Stello, Mississippi. As the seventh child of eighteen children, Natha had to begin caring for her younger siblings at an early age. She soon discovered that she had a gift for cooking. Her earliest memory of creating great meals was watching her mother plan and prepares meals for a very large family. Growing up impoverished in the deep south in the 1930's, meal preparation consisted of fresh foods that could be grown in gardens and raised on the farm Good eating to say the least.
She states "we didn't have a lot of choices; we simply had to eat what was in the kitchen."

Natha became a master in the kitchen. She quickly learned how to use "what was in the kitchen" and create tempting, delicious and healthy meals. When seeking a career, Natha was told by an elderly woman in her community that there were two things that would always be needed; medical care and food preparation (cooking). Mrs. Parker obviously chose cooking.

Over a forty year period, Natha was a domestic worker, doing housework and cooking. She also spent many of those years working as a cook in various cafes and restaurants. Her skills in the kitchen are unparalleled.

Natha was married to the late J. P. Parker for 41 years until his death in 1980. To this union ten children were born: Jesse (deceased), Roy, Mattie, Dorothy, Helen, Deloris, John (deceased), Cormac (deceased), Curtis and Alice. Natha is affectionately known as "Little Mama" to her 25 Grand children and 26 Great Grand children. As a devoted wife and mother, Natha has always dedicated her life to providing for the needs of her family. Even though her children are grown and some of their children have children, she still is the glue that holds her family together; in good times and bad times.

In 1984, Natha moved to Vallejo, California to live with one of her daughters (Deloris). She immediately became involved with church and community activities. As a member of the Friendship Baptist Church, Natha was active with the Home Mission, singles ministry and of course, the kitchen committee. She also volunteered weekly for the Meals On Wheels Project.

Natha currently lives in Sacramento, California. She does volunteer work three days per week in the kitchen of the Samuel Pannell Community Center. As a member of Genesis Missionary Baptist Church she serves on the Mothers Board and was a member of the culinary committee from 1991 - 1997. Other community service projects that Natha has been involved in include: The Age Concern where she volunteered for three years preparing meals and providing companionship for senior citizens. Her life emanates service to her faith, family and community.

When asked why at the age of 75 she still feels a need to give service to her community, she states "I feel that God has given me a talent (cooking) and it should be used to help others. It brings me joy to give service."

In her golden years, Natha has become a constant traveler. She has been to most of the fifty states and also has visited many foreign countries, including: Japan, Germany, France, Spain, Italy, England and Holland. The highlight of her travels was a trip to the Holy Land that she completed in 1995.

As of the writing of this 14th Anniversary Edition, Natha has moved back to the state of Mississippi to enjoy the company of her children, grandchildren, great-grand children and great, great-grandchildren.

Angel Biscuits

INGREDIENTS:

5 cups **flour**
1 teaspoon **baking soda**
1/4 cup **sugar**
1 package **yeast**
2 cups **buttermilk**
1-1/2 teaspoon **salt**
1 teaspoon **baking powder**
1 cup **shortening**
3 tablespoons warm **water**

PROCEDURE:

1. Sift dry ingredients (except yeast) together.
2. Add shortening.
3. Dissolve yeast in warm water and pour in buttermilk
4. Add dry ingredients to liquid and mix well.
5. Roll dough and cut into biscuits.
6. Bake on ungreased cooking sheet for 10-12 minutes at 425 degrees.

NATHA'S TIP: This dough will last up to 1-2 days in the refrigerator, if covered.

"Whoso diggeth a pit shall fall therein: and he that rolleth a stone it will return upon him."

~*Proverbs 26:27*

Angel Corn Sticks

INGREDIENTS:

1-1/2 cups **corn meal**
1 cup all purpose **flour**
1 package **dry yeast**
1 tablespoon **sugar**
1 teaspoon **salt**
1/2 cup **vegetable oil**

2 cups **buttermilk**
2 **eggs** (beaten)
1-1/2 teaspoon **baking soda**
1 teaspoon **baking powder**

PROCEDURE:

1. Combine corn meal, flour, yeast, sugar, salt, baking powder, baking soda in a large mixing bowl.
2. In a separate bowl, combine eggs, buttermilk, and oil.
3. Add this mixture to dry ingredients stirring until batter is smooth.
4. Spoon batter into well greased cast iron (or aluminum) corn stick pans, filling half full.
5. Bake at 450 degrees for 12 to 15 minutes.

Yields approximately 3 dozen corn sticks.

"If we suffer we shall also reign with Him. If we deny Him, He also will deny us."

~2 Timothy 2:12

Baking Powder Biscuits

INGREDIENTS:

2 cups sifted **flour**
3 teaspoons **baking powder**
1/2 teaspoon **salt**
4 tablespoons **butter/margarine**
3/4 cup **milk**

PROCEDURE:

1. Sift dry ingredients together.
2. Add butter; mix with a fork or blender with dough hooks.
3. Add milk to make a soft dough.
4. Toss lightly on a floured board until surface is smooth.
5. Roll out 1/2 inch thick and cut with floured biscuit cutter.
6. Bake at 450 degrees in a well greased pan for about 12 minutes.

"A man's heart deviseth his way: but the Lord directeth his steps."
~Proverbs 16:9

Can't Fail Rolls

INGREDIENTS:

3-1/2 cups **flour**
2 tablespoons **sugar**
1 package **dry yeast**
1 cup of warm **water**

1 **egg** (well beaten)
2 tablespoons melted **shortening**
1 teaspoon **salt**

PROCEDURE:

1. Mix dry ingredients.
2. Dissolve yeast in warm water and pour into dry ingredients.
3. Add melted shortening and egg. Mix well.
4. Let stand one (1) hour.
5. Knead, shape into rolls and allow to rise for forty five (45) minutes.
6. Bake at 450 degrees until golden brown.

"To whom much is given, from him much will be required."
~Luke 12:48

Natha's Dinner Rolls

INGREDIENTS:

2 cups warm **water**
2 packages **dry yeast**
1 tablespoon **salt**
5 cups **flour**
1 cup cold **water**

1 cup **sugar**
2 **eggs**
1 cup melted **shortening**

PROCEDURE:

1. Dissolve yeast in 1/2 cup of warm water
2. Stir in remaining water, salt and 3 cups of flour mix well
3. Leave covered for 2 hours
4. Add melted shortening, beat well with mixer
5. Continue to beat, add eggs, sugar and cold water
6. Stir in enough flour to make stiff dough
7. Cover, let rise until double in size
8. Make into rolls, let rise again until double in size
9. Bake at 400 degrees for 20-25 minutes

Add butter, jelly etc. and enjoy

NATHA'S TIP: This dough will keep in refrigerator 1-2 days, if covered.

"The Lord is my shepherd, I shall not want."

~Psalms 23:1

Pancakes From Scratch

INGREDIENTS:

1 cup **flour**
1 tablespoon **sugar**
1 **egg**
1/2 teaspoon **salt**

1 cup **milk**
2 tablespoons melted **butter**
1/4 teaspoon **vanilla flavor**

PROCEDURE:

1. Combine all ingredients.
2. Mix until smooth.
3. Cook in a medium size well greased frying pan

NATHA'S TIP: Be sure to use medium low heat and turn cakes over often so as not to burn.

"Fear thou not, for I am with thee: be not dismayed; for I am thy God: I will strengthen thee; yea, I will help thee; yea, I will uphold thee with the right hand of my righteousness."

~Isaiah 41:10

Quick Buttermilk Biscuits

INGREDIENTS:

1/2 cup **butter or margarine**
3/4 cup **buttermilk**
2 cups **self-rising flour**

PROCEDURE:

1. Mix butter and flour.
2. Add buttermilk to make a soft dough.
3. Mix well.
4. Roll on floured sheet.
5. Cut into biscuits.
6. Bake on a lightly greased cooking sheet at 425 degrees for 12 minutes or until golden brown.

"In the beginning God created the heaven and the earth."
~Genesis 1:1

Quick Muffins

INGREDIENTS:

2 cups sifted **flour**
1/4 cup **sugar**
1/2 teaspoon **salt**
3 teaspoons **baking powder**

1 **egg**
1 cup **milk**
1/4 cup melted **butter or margarine**

PROCEDURE:

1. Melt butter or margarine, set aside to cool.
2. Sift dry ingredients in mixing bowl.
3. Add egg, milk and cooled butter/margarine, mix well.
4. Grease 1 dozen capacity muffin pan.
5. Fill each slot of greased muffin pan 2/3 full.
6. Bake at 425 degrees for 20 minutes or until brown.

Yields 1 dozen muffins.

"Come unto me all ye that labour and are heavy laden and I will give you rest"

~Matthew 11:28

Scratch Cornbread

INGREDIENTS:

1 cup **yellow cornmeal**
1 cup **flour**
2 tablespoons **sugar**
1 teaspoon **salt**
1 cup **milk**
1 **egg** (beaten)

1/3 cup **shortening**
1 tablespoon **baking powder**

PROCEDURE:

1. Combine all dry ingredients in bowl and mix well.
2. Add shortening.
3. Beat egg and milk together. Mix with other ingredients and blend.
4. Pour into well buttered 8-inch pan.
5. Bake at 400 degrees for 25 minutes or until done.

After cooking, spread butter on top of bread while still hot. Enjoy.

"Blessed are those who hunger and thirst for righteousness, for they shall be filled."

~Matthew 5:6

Southern Cornbread #1

INGREDIENTS:

2-1/2 cups **yellow corn meal**
1/2 teaspoon **baking soda**
1 teaspoon **salt**
3 teaspoons **cooking oil**
2 **eggs** (beaten)
2 cups **buttermilk**

PROCEDURE:

1. Combine all dry ingredients in a large mixing bowl.
2. Add beaten eggs, oil and buttermilk.
3. Beat until batter in smooth.
4. Pour batter into a well greased 9 inch square pan.
5. Bake at 400 degrees for 30 to 35 minutes:

NATHA'S TIP: Never put sugar in southern corn bread.

"For what is a man profited, if he shall gain the whole world, and loses his own soul?"

~Matthew 16:26

Southern Cornbread #2

INGREDIENTS:

1-2/3 cups **yellow corn meal**
1/3 cup **flour**
3 teaspoons **baking powder**
4 tablespoons **cooking oil**
1 teaspoon **salt**
1 **egg** (beaten)
1 cup **milk**

PROCEDURE:

1. Sift all dry ingredients in a large bowl.
2. Add beaten egg, milk and oil.
3. Mix just enough to moisten dry ingredients.
4. Pour batter into buttered 9 inch square pan.
5. Bake at 400 degrees for 25 to 30 minutes.

NATHA'S TIP: Never put sugar in southern corn bread.

"Have mercy upon me. O God, according to thy loving kindness: according unto the multitude of thy tender mercies blot out my transgressions. Wash me thoroughly from mine iniquity, and cleanse me from my sin."

~Psalm 51:1-2

Big Pound Cake

INGREDIENTS:

3 cups **sugar**
1-1/2 cups **shortening**
6 **eggs**
1 cup self **rising flou**r
1-1/2 cups **milk**
2 teaspoons **vanilla or lemon flavor**
3-1/2 cups **cake flour**

PROCEDURE:

1. Cream shortening and sugar.
2. Add eggs one at a time mix well.
3. Add all other ingredients a small amount at time, mix well.
4. Place batter in a large greased and floured cake pan.
5. Place in a cold oven.
6. Set oven at 325 degrees and cook for 1-1/2 hour.
7. Let cool in pan for 10 minutes then place on a cake plate or rack to complete cooling .

"A good name is rather to be chosen than great riches, and loving favor rather than silver and gold."

~Proverbs 22:1

Butter Pound Cake

INGREDIENTS:

1 pound soft **butter**
1 pound **powdered sugar**
3 cups **cake flour**
6 large **eggs**

PROCEDURE:

1. Mix butter with sugar.
2. Add eggs one at a time.
3. Add flour one cup at a time. Mix well.
4. Pour into greased and floured cake pan.
5. Bake at 325 degrees for 1 hour and 15 minutes.

"Thy Word I have hidden in mine heart that I might not sin against Thee"

~Psalms 119:11

Buttermilk Pound Cake

INGREDIENTS:

5 **eggs**
1-1/2 cup **shortening**
1 cup **buttermilk**
1/4 teaspoon **baking soda**
1 tablespoon boiling **water**
3 cups **sugar**

1 teaspoon **vanilla flavor**
3-1/2 cups **cake flour**

PROCEDURE:

1. Cream shortening and sugar together.
2. Add eggs one at a time mixing batter well after each.
3. Mix baking soda with tablespoon of boiling water stir well; add to sugar, shortening and eggs.
4. Add flour and buttermilk alternatively to mixture.
5. Mix well until batter is very smooth.
6. Add flavor, continue to mix for an additional three (3) minutes.
7. Pour mixture into well greased and floured cake pan and bake at 325 degrees for 1-1/2 hours.

"The Lord knowest them that are His."

~2 Timothy 2:19

Buttermilk Tea Cakes

INGREDIENTS:

1 cup **shortening**
1-1/2 cups **sugar**
3 **eggs**
4 cups plain **flour**
1 teaspoon **baking powder**
1 teaspoon **baking soda**

1/2 teaspoon **salt**
1/4 cup **buttermilk**
1-1/4 teaspoons **vanilla flavor**

PROCEDURE:

1. Mix all ingredients well.
2. Cover and chill one hour.
3. Roll dough and cut into cookies.
4. Place on a lightly greased cooking sheet and cook at 350 degrees for 10-15 minutes.

"To everything there is a season, and a time to every purpose under the heaven."

~Ecclesiastes 3:1

Coconut-Pecan Filling And Frosting

INGREDIENTS:

1 cup **evaporated milk**
1 cup **sugar**
3 **egg** yolks, slightly beaten
1/2 cup **butter or margarine**
1 teaspoon **vanilla**

1 1/3 cups **coconut**
1 cup chopped **pecan**

PROCEDURE:

1. Combine milk, sugar, egg yolks, butter and vanilla in saucepan.
2. Cook and stir over medium heat until mixture thicken.
3. Remove from heat.
4. Add coconut and pecans.
5. Cool until spreading consistency, beating occasionally.

"Boast not thyself of tomorrow, for thou knowest not what a day may bring forth."

~Proverbs 27:1

German Chocolate Cake

INGREDIENTS:

4 ounces **sweet chocolate**
2-1/3 cups sifted **cake flour**
1-1/2 cups **sugar**
1 teaspoon **baking soda**
1/2 teaspoon **baking powder**
Coconut-Pecan Filling and Frosting

1/2 teaspoon **salt**
2/3 cup **butter/margarine**
1 cup **buttermilk**
1 teaspoon **vanilla**
2 **eggs**

PROCEDURE:

1. Melt chocolate over low heat; cool.
2. Sift flour with sugar, baking soda, baking powder and salt.
3. Stir butter in mixer bowl to soften.
4. Add flour mixture, 3/4 cup of buttermilk and vanilla.
5. Mix to dampen flour; beat 2 minutes at medium speed of electric mixer,
6. scraping bowl occasionally.
7. Add melted chocolate, eggs and remaining buttermilk. Beat 1 minute longer.
8. Pour batter into three 8-ince layer pans, lined on bottoms with wax paper.
9. Bake at 350 degrees for 30-35 minutes, or cake tester inserted into centers come out clean.
10. Cool in pans for 15-20 minutes; remove from pans and cool on racks.
11. Spread filling on layers and stack.

"Fret not thyself because of evildoers, neither be thou envious against the workers of iniquity."

~Psalms 37: 1

Good Pound Cake

INGREDIENTS:

2 sticks **butter**
2 tablespoons **shortening**
3 cups **sugar**
3 cups **flour**
1 teaspoon **baking powder**
1 teaspoon **vanilla flavor**
2 teaspoons **lemon flavor**
5 large **eggs**
1 cup **milk**

PROCEDURE:

1. Cream butter and shortening with sugar.
2. Add eggs one at a time, mix well.
3. Combine flour with baking powder.
4. Add dry ingredients to other mixture alternately with milk. Blend well.
5. Add flavor.
6. Pour into well greased and floured cake pan. Bake at 325 degrees for one hour and fifteen minutes.

"The things which are impossible with men are possible with God."

~Luke 18:27

Good Sugar Cookies

INGREDIENTS:

2 **eggs**
1 cup **vegetable oil**
1 cup **sugar**
1 cup **powder sugar**
2 sticks of **butter**
5 cups plain **flour**

1 teaspoon **baking powder**
1/4 teaspoon **salt**
1 teaspoon **cream of tartar**
2 teaspoons of **vanilla flavor**

PROCEDURE:

1. Cream butter.
2. Add oil, sugar, powder sugar and eggs.
3. Add vanilla flavor and mix well.
4. Sift all dry ingredients together and add to above ingredients.
5. Roll dough into ball about the size of a walnut and place on lightly greased cooking sheet one inch apart.
6. Flatten ball with the bottom a glass that has been dipped in sugar.
7. Bake at 350 degrees for 10 minutes or until lightly brown.

"Judge not, that ye be not judged. For with what judgment ye judge, ye shall be judged: and with what measure ye mete, it shall be measured to you again."

~Matthew 7:1-2

Natha's Favorite Pie Crust

INGREDIENTS:

3 cups **flour**
1-1/2 cups **shortening**
1/2 teaspoon **salt**
5 tablespoons cold **water**
1 tablespoon **vinegar**
1 **egg**

PROCEDURE:

1. Combine shortening, salt and flour, mix well.
2. Beat egg, add water and vinegar.
3. Add this to the flour mixture a little at time, mixing well.
4. Roll dough in to a ball and then divide into four portions.

This will make four (4) single pie shells.

"Watch ye and pray, let ye enter into temptation. The spirit truly is ready but the flesh is weak."

~Mark 14: 38

Never Fail Pie Crust

INGREDIENTS:

4 cups of **flour**
1 tablespoon **sugar**
3 teaspoons **salt**
1 **egg**
1-3/4 cup **shortening**
1/2 cup **water**
1 tablespoon **vinegar**

PROCEDURE:

1. Mix flour, sugar and salt in bowl.
2. Add shortening and mix well.
3. Beat egg and combine with vinegar and water.
4. Add to flour mixture to moisten.
5. Divide dough into five (5) balls ready for rolling.
6. Chill for 30 minutes before using.
7. After chilling, roll out on greased pie plates.

This recipe will make approximately five (5) nine inch pie crusts.

NATHA'S TIP: Unused dough can be stored in freezer. When ready to use, thaw and roll out on pie plate.

"Be doers of the Word, and not hearers only deceiving you own selves."

~James 1:22

Old Fashioned Apple Pie

INGREDIENTS:

1 cup **sugar**
4 tablespoons **flour**
1 teaspoon **cinnamon**
1/4 teaspoon **salt**
6 tart **apples** (sliced thin)
2 tablespoons **butter or margarine**

PROCEDURE:

1. Gently mix all ingredients together in a large bowl.
2. Add cinnamon as last ingredient.
3. Pour into an 8 inch pastry shell, dot with two tablespoons of butter or margarine.
4. Add top crust.
5. Bake at 425 degrees for 10 minutes.
6. Reduce heat to 350 degrees and continue to bake until golden brown.

"Remember now thy Creator in the days of thy youth, while the evil days come not, nor the years draw nigh, when thou shall say, I have no pleasure in them."

~*Ecclesiastes 12:1*

Old Fashioned Lemon Pie

INGREDIENTS:

2 tablespoons **flour**
1 cup **sugar**
1-1/2 cups of **milk**
2 tablespoons **butter**
3 tablespoons **lemon juice**

3 teaspoons grated **lemon rind**
2 **eggs**

PROCEDURE:

1. Mix milk, flour, sugar, lemon juice, lemon rind and butter.
2. Separate eggs.
3. Beat yolks and add to mixture, mix well.
4. Beat egg whites and fold into mixture.
5. Pour into a 9 inch uncooked pastry shell.
6. Place on bottom of hot oven and bake at 450 degrees for 10 minutes.
7. Move to middle oven rack, reduce heat to 350 degrees and bake an additional 40 minutes.

"I came not to call the righteous but sinners to repentance."
~Luke 5:32

Seven Up Pound Cake

INGREDIENTS:

3 cups **flour**
1/4 teaspoon **salt**
5 large **eggs**
3 cups **sugar**
1 cup **butter**
1/2 cup **vegetable shortening**

1-1/2 teaspoons **vanilla flavor**
1/2 teaspoon **lemon flavor**
1 cup **7 up**

PROCEDURE:

1. Combine flour and salt, set aside.
2. Combine sugar, butter and shortening.
3. Add eggs one at a time.
4. Add dry ingredients alternately with 7 up.
5. Mix well.
6. Add flavor.
7. Pour mixture into a well greased and floured cake pan.
8. Bake for 1-1/2 hours at 350 degrees.

NATHA'S TIP:
For best results with this recipe preheat oven at 325 degrees then set at 350 degrees for baking.

"In the beginning was the Word, and the Word was with God, and the Word was God. The same was in the beginning with God."
~John 1:1-2

Swedish Tea Cakes

INGREDIENTS:

1/2 cup **powdered sugar**
1 cup soft **butter or margarine**
2 teaspoons **vanilla flavor**
2 cups **all purpose flour**
1 cup finely chopped **pecans**
1/4 teaspoon **salt**

PROCEDURE:

1. Combine sugar, margarine and vanilla in a large bowl, mix well.
2. Add flour, salt and pecans.
3. Mix until dough holds together.
4. Shape dough into 1 inch balls and place about an inch apart on an ungreased cookie sheet.
5. Bake at 325 degrees for 15-20 minutes.
6. Remove from cookie sheet.
7. Cool slightly and roll in powdered sugar.
8. Cool completely and roll in powdered sugar again.

Note: You will need to have additional powdered sugar to roll cooked tea cakes.

"And whatsoever ye do in word or deed, do all in the name of the Lord Jesus, giving thanks to God and the Father by him."
                                            ~Colossians 3:1

Sweet Potato Pie #1

INGREDIENTS:

2 **eggs**
1 cup **sugar**
1/2 teaspoon **salt**
1/8 teaspoon grounded **nutmeg**
1 teaspoon **cinnamon**
1 cup **milk**

2 tablespoons **butter**
1-1/2 cup mashed cooked **sweet potatoes**

PROCEDURE:

1. Combine sugar, nutmeg and cinnamon, mix well.
2. Stir in sweet potatoes.
3. Add milk, beaten eggs, butter and salt.
4. Mix until smooth.
5. Pour mixture into pie shell and bake.

Note: If using an aluminum pie baking dish, bake 1 hour at 375 degrees. If you prefer a glass baking dish, bake 1 hour at 350 degrees.

"And ye shall know the truth, and the truth shall make you free."
~John 8:32

Sweet Potato Pie #2

INGREDIENTS:

3/4 cup **sugar**
1/8 teaspoon **nutmeg**
1/4 teaspoon **cinnamon**
1-1/4 cups cooked **sweet potatoes**
1 cup evaporated **milk**

2 **eggs** (beaten)
3 tablespoons melted **butter**
1 teaspoon **vanilla**

PROCEDURE:

1. Combine sugar, nutmeg, and cinnamon.
2. Stir in potatoes.
3. Add milk, beaten eggs, butter and vanilla.
4. Mix until smooth.
5. Pour mixture into pie shell and bake.

Note: If using an aluminum pie baking dish, bake 1 hour at 375 degrees. If you prefer a glass baking dish, bake 1 hour at 350 degrees.

"For all have sinned, and come short of the glory of God."
~Roman 3:23

Tea Cakes

INGREDIENTS:

3 **eggs**
1-1/2 cups **sugar**
1 stick **margarine**
1/4 cup **cooking oil**
2 teaspoons **vanilla flavor**

1 teaspoon **ginger**
3 cups **self-rising flour**

PROCEDURE:

1. Combine sugar and margarine, mix well.
2. Add eggs one at time, mix well.
3. Add flour and cooking oil alternately.
4. Add ginger and vanilla, mix well on medium speed.
5. Roll dough.
6. Cut in to cookies whatever size that you desire.
7. Bake on a lightly greased cooking sheet at 350 degrees for 10-15 minutes until brown.

"That if thou shalt confess with thy mouth the Lord Jesus, and shall believe in thine heart that God hath raised him from the dead, thou shalt be saved."

~Roman 10:9

Two Egg Layer Cake

INGREDIENTS:

2 **eggs**
1/2 cup **shortening**
1-1/2 cups **sugar**
2 -1/4 cups sifted **cake flour**
2-1/2 teaspoons **baking powder**

1 teaspoon **salt**
1 cup + 2 tablespoon **milk**

PROCEDURE:

1. Mix shortening and sugar in a large mixing bowl
2. Add eggs one at a time
3. Mix flour, baking powder and salt together in a separate bowl
4. Add this mixture to shortening, sugar and eggs alternately with milk
5. Pour mixture into two (2) 9 x 11 inch round pans, lined with wax paper
6. Place in oven and bake at 375 degrees for 25-30 minutes until done
7. Add frosting of your choice

NATHA'S TIP:
If you want a large cake, this receipt can be doubled.

"Train up a child in the way he should go: and when he is old, he will not depart from it."

~*Proverbs 22:6*

Deviled Eggs

INGREDIENTS:

4 hard boiled **eggs**
2 teaspoons **mayonnaise**
1 teaspoon **lemon juice**
1/4 teaspoon grated **onion**
1/8 teaspoon **pepper**

1/2 teaspoon **dry mustard**
1/2 teaspoon **Worcestershire sauce**
1/2 teaspoon **salt**
1/2 teaspoon **paprika**

PROCEDURE:

1. Cut eggs in halves lengthwise.
2. Remove yoke.
3. Mash yoke, add mayonnaise, lemon juice, onion, mustard, Worcestershire sauce, salt and pepper
4. Beat until fluffy.
5. Refill egg whites.
6. Garnish with paprika.

"There hath ho temptation taken you but such as is common to man: but God is faithful, who will not suffer you to be tempted above that ye are able; but will with the temptation also make a way to escape, that ye may be able to bear it."

~*I Corinthians 10:13*

Deviled Eggs With Pimiento

INGREDIENTS:

6 hard boiled **eggs**
1/4 cup **salad dressing**
1 teaspoon **mustard**
1/4 teaspoon **salt**

1 teaspoon **parsley**
1 teaspoon **pimiento**

PROCEDURE:

1. Cut eggs in half.
2. Remove yoke.
3. Mash yoke and blend in salad dressing, mustard and salt.
4. Refill egg white.
5. Garnish with parsley and pimiento.

"Cast thy burden upon the Lord, and he shall sustain thee: he shall never suffer the righteous to be moved."

~Psalms 55: 22

Picnic Eggs

INGREDIENTS:

4 hard boiled **eggs**
1/3 cup grated **parmesan cheese**
1 teaspoon **mustard**
1/4 teaspoon **pepper**
1/4 cup **milk**

PROCEDURE:

1. Cut egg in halves lengthwise.
2. Remove yolks.
3. Add cheese, mustard, pepper and enough milk to moisten.
4. Beat until fluffy.
5. Refill egg white.
6. Chill in refrigerator until ready to serve.

"Therefore, my beloved brethren, be ye steadfast, unmovable, always abounding in the work of the Lord, for as much as ye know that your labor is not in vain in the Lord."

~I Corinthians 15:58

Scrambled Eggs

INGREDIENTS:

2 tablespoons **margarine**
6 **eggs** (beaten)
1/3 cup **milk**
1/2 teaspoon **salt**
1/4 teaspoon **pepper**
1/4 cup **sharp cheddar cheese**

PROCEDURE:

1. Melt margarine in skillet over low heat.
2. Combine eggs, milk and seasonings.
3. Pour in skillet.
4. Cook slowly, stirring occasionally until eggs are done.
5. Sprinkle with cheese and serve.

Great dish for breakfast, lunch or dinner.

"And He sat down, and called the twelve and saith unto them, if anyone desires to be first, he shall be last of all and servant of all."
~Mark 9:35

Barbecued Baby Back Ribs

INGREDIENTS:

1 tablespoon **celery seeds**
1 tablespoon **chili powder**
1/4 cup **brown sugar**
1 tablespoon **salt**
1 teaspoon **paprika**

1/4 cup **vinegar**
1 - 8 oz cans **tomato sauce**
2-1/2 pounds **baby back ribs**

PROCEDURE:

1. Combine celery seeds, chili powder, brown sugar, salt and paprika.
2. Rub 1/3 of this mixture on ribs.
3. Combine rest of mixture with tomato sauce and vinegar.
4. Simmer this mixture on very low heat.
5. Cook ribs in oven on broil or over hot coals on barbecue grill.
6. As ribs are cooking baste occasionally with sauce.

"For ye know the grace of our Lord Jesus Christ, that, though he was rich, yet for your sakes he became poor, that ye through his poverty might be rich."

~II Corinthians 8:9

Beef Stew From Scratch

INGREDIENTS:

2 pounds **stew meat**
1 large **turnip** (root portion)
2 large **carrots**
1 large **onion** (chopped)
8 oz. can **tomato paste**

6 medium **potatoes**
1 tablespoon **flour**
1 tablespoon **butter**
2 cups **water**
salt and pepper to your taste

PROCEDURE:

1. Cut beef into 1 inch cubes.
2. Place in heavy saucepan with 2 cups of water, cook until almost done.
3. Peel potatoes.
4. Cut potatoes, carrots and turnips in 2 inch cubes, add to meat.
5. Add chopped onions.
6. Cook until done.
7. Add butter and flour together to make a paste, add this to meat and vegetables.
8. Add tomatoes paste, salt and pepper to taste.
9. Simmer for 10 minutes.

Note: If mixture is too thick add additional water to obtain the proper consistency.

"The Lord is my light and my salvation; whom shall I fear? The Lord is the strength of my life; of whom shall I be afraid?"
                                                                              ~Psalm 27:1

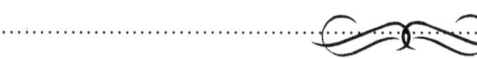

Buttermilk Fried Chicken

INGREDIENTS:

1 **Fryer**, cut up
Seasoned Flour
Buttermilk
Cooking Oil

PROCEDURE:

1. Dip chicken pieces in buttermilk, then in seasoned flour.
2. Repeat this step.
3. Chill in refrigerator for one hour so that coating will adhere to chicken.
4. Fry in cooking oil until golden brown.

NATHA'S TIP: If baking is preferred, place chicken in a shallow pan and bake at 450 degrees for 45 minutes to one hour.

"I will declare thy name unto my brethren: in the midst of the congregation will I praise thee."

~Psalm 22:22

Chicken & Dumplings

INGREDIENTS:

2 cups sifted **flour**
2 teaspoons **baking powder**
1 teaspoon **salt**
1/3 cup **butter or shortening**
1/2 cup **milk**

1 **chicken** (cut up & boiled)
4 cups **chicken stock**

PROCEDURE:

1. Combine sifted flour, salt and baking powder.
2. Mix in shortening with dry ingredients.
3. Add milk to make stiff dough.
4. Take a small amount of dough, roll thin and cut into 1-1/2 inch strips.
5. Repeat this process until you have desired amount of strips.
6. Add strips to boiling chicken stock.
7. Add seasonings and butter.
8. Add chicken parts.
9. Cover and simmer for 30 minutes.

NATHA'S TIP: Try this dish with some southern corn bread.

"Stand fast therefore in the liberty wherewith Christ hath made us free, and be not entangled again with the yoke of bondage."
~Galatians 5:1

Chicken Gumbo

INGREDIENTS:

1-1/2 pound **chicken**
1 cup **lima beans**
2 teaspoons **salt**
1/2 teaspoon **pepper**
6 quarts **water**
1-1/2 pounds sliced **okra**

1 medium **onion** (sliced)
2 cups uncooked **corn**
2 tablespoons **butter**
6 medium **tomatoes**
4 cup uncooked **rice**

PROCEDURE:

1. Cut chicken into serving portions.
2. Simmer with lima beans and seasonings.
3. Fry okra, onion and corn in butter until light brown.
4. Add tomatoes.
5. Add vegetables and rice to chicken and cook until tender.

Serves 10-14.

"By grace you have been saved through faith and that not of yourselves; it is the gift of God."

~Ephesians 2:8

Chicken With Vegetables

INGREDIENTS:

1 **chicken**, cut up
1 small **green pepper**, diced
1 can **cream of mushroom soup**
1 **red bell pepper**, diced
1 pkg. frozen **peas & carrots**

1/2 cup **water**
salt and pepper to taste

PROCEDURE:

1. Place chicken in a baking dish.
2. Cover with foil and cook at 350 degrees until brown.
3. Combine soup, water, frozen vegetables and peppers.
4. Pour mixture over chicken and continue to cook at 350 degrees until vegetables are done.

Serve over rice or mashed potatoes.

"The earth is the Lord's, and the fullness thereof; the world, and they that dwell therein."

~Psalm 24:1

Chili For The Crowd

INGREDIENTS:

2 pounds of **coarse ground beef**
1 tablespoon **chili powder**
2 teaspoons **salt**
1 teaspoon **sugar**
1-1/2 cups chopped **onion**
1-1/2 cups minced **green peppers** drained

2 (15 oz) cans **tomato sauce**
1 cup **water**
1 clove **garlic** (crushed)
1/2 teaspoon **ground cumin**
1 (1 lb. 14 oz) can small **red beans**

PROCEDURE:

1. Cook meat in Dutch oven of heavy kettle until it loses redness.
2. Sprinkle with chili powder, salt and sugar; blend well through meat.
3. Add onion and green pepper.
4. Cook, stirring occasionally, until vegetables soften.
5. Add Tomato Sauce, water, garlic and cumin.
6. Simmer uncovered 1 to 1-1/2 hour.
7. Add beans, simmer uncovered 1/2 hour or until desired consistency.

Makes 2-1/2 quarts.

"Is anything too hard for the Lord?"

~Genesis 18:14

German Style Beef Stew

INGREDIENTS:

1-1/4 pound **stew meat**
1 medium **onion**, diced
2 **carrots**, peeled & cut into chunks
1/2 cup **milk**
1-1/2 cups **water**
2 tablespoons **ketchup**

2 tablespoons **margarine**
2 tablespoons **flour**
salt and pepper to taste

PROCEDURE:

1. Brown meat on all sides in margarine in a large skillet.
2. Add onions and brown lightly.
3. Add 1-1/2 cups water and salt and pepper to taste.
4. Add ketchup.
5. Bring to a boil, cover and simmer until meat is almost tender.
6. Add vegetables and cook for twenty minutes or until done.
7. Blend milk and flour and stir into mixture.
8. Cook, stirring until slightly thickened.

Serve with cornbread for a delicious all in one meal.

"This is the day the Lord has made; we will rejoice and be glad in it."

~Psalm 118:24

Glorified Bake Beans

INGREDIENTS:

1 pound **ground meat**
1 **onion** (chopped)
1 **green bell pepper**
1 clove **garlic**
1 large **can of pork and beans**
1/2 cup **ketchup**
3 tablespoons **brown sugar**
1 tablespoon **Worcestershire**
1/2 teaspoon prepared **mustard**

PROCEDURE:

1. Brown and drain ground meat.
2. Chop onion, bell pepper and garlic.
3. Sauté chopped vegetables in butter or margarine.
4. Combine beans, ketchup, brown sugar, mustard and Worcestershire sauce in large baking dish.
5. Add onion, bell pepper and garlic and brown meat.
6. Bake at 350 degrees until mixture is bubbly.

Serve with green salad and garlic bread.

"Rejoice in the Lord always: and again I say, Rejoice."
~Philippians 4:4

Potatoes & Ham

INGREDIENTS:

1/4 cup **margarine**
1/4 cup **all purpose flour**
2-1/2 cups **milk**
1 teaspoon **salt**
1/2 teaspoon **dry mustard**
1/4 teaspoon **pepper**

2 cups **sharp cheddar cheese** (shredded)
2 cups chopped cooked **ham**
2 tablespoons chopped **onion**
6 cups sliced, cooked **potatoes**

PROCEDURE:

1. In a double boiler, combine flour, milk, margarine and seasonings.
2. Add 1-1/2 cups cheese, stirring until melted.
3. Add ham and onion.
4. Watch and stir constantly to avoid burning.
5. Alternately layer potatoes and cheese sauce in a 2 quart casserole dish.
6. At this juncture only use about 1/2 of the cheese sauce.
7. Bake at 350 degrees for 15 minutes.
8. Remove from oven and top with remaining cheese (1/2 cup) and return to oven until cheese begins to melt.
9. Remove from oven and serve.

NATHA'S TIP: This dish is excellent with scratch corn bread.

"The steps of a good man are ordered by Lord: and he delighteth in his way."

~Psalm 37:23

Turkey Hash

INGREDIENTS:

1/2 cup **butter**
1/2 cup **flour**
4 cups **milk**
3 cups diced cooked **turkey**
1/2 cup diced cooked **carrots**
1/2 cup diced cooked **potatoes**
1/2 cup diced cooked **celery**
salt and pepper to taste

PROCEDURE:

1. Mix all ingredients together.
2. Pour in a butter greased casserole dish.
3. Bake at 350 degrees until mixture bubbles.
4. Sprinkle with parmesan cheese.

"Oh, the depth of the riches both of the wisdom and knowledge of God, how unsearchable are His judgments, and His ways past finding out!"

~Romans 11:33

Chicken Salad

INGREDIENTS:

2 cups cubed cooked **chicken**
1 cup chopped **celery**
1/4 cup chopped **pickles**
1 chopped hardboiled **egg**
1/2 cup **mayonnaise**
1 tablespoon **lemon juice**

1/2 teaspoon **season salt**
1/2 teaspoon **dry mustard**
1/8 teaspoon **nutmeg**
1/4 teaspoon **salt**
1/8 teaspoon **white pepper**

PROCEDURE:

1. Toss chicken with celery, pickle and egg.
2. Combine mayonnaise, lemon juice and all seasonings, mix well.
3. Add to chicken.
4. Serve on crisp lettuce, sprinkle with paprika if you choose.

NATHA'S TIP: This salad can also be used for sandwiches.

"Wait on the Lord: be of good courage, and he shall strengthen thine heart: wait, I say, on the Lord."

~Psalm 27:14

Cole Slaw With Color

INGREDIENTS:

1 medium **green cabbage** (shredded)
1 small **purple cabbage** (shredded)
3 shredded **carrots**
1/2 cup **mayonnaise**
2 tablespoons **sweet pickle relish**
3 tablespoons **milk**

PROCEDURE:

1. Combine mayonnaise, sugar and milk.
2. Pour over other ingredients .
3. Refrigerate for at least 1 hour before serving

NATHA'S TIP: To get the best taste from this slaw, leave in the refrigerator overnight before serving. This allows the ingredients to set.

"Blessed is he that considereth the poor: The Lord will deliver him in time of trouble."

~Psalm 41:1

English Pea Salad

INGREDIENTS:

1 can **English peas** (drained)
1 cup **cheese** (cubed)
2 hard boiled **eggs** (chopped)
1 teaspoon **salt**
1/2 cup **mayonnaise**
1 teaspoon **pepper**

1/2 medium **onion** (chopped)
3 tablespoons diced **bell pepper**
1 ripe **tomato** (diced)

PROCEDURE:

1. Combine all ingredients except mayonnaise, mix well.
2. Gently add mayonnaise to coat other ingredients.

"Fret not thyself because of evildoers, neither be thou envious against the workers of iniquity. For they shall soon be cut down like the grass, and wither as the green herb."

~Psalm 37:1-2

Macaroni Salad

INGREDIENTS:

3 cups cooked **Elbow Macaroni**
2 tablespoons chopped **onion**
1 cup **salad dressing**
1 cup cubed **American cheese**

PROCEDURE:

1. Combine macaroni, onion, and cheese.
2. Moisten with mayonnaise or salad dressing.
3. Serve on lettuce or watercress.

NATHA'S TIP: If you have a large gathering, this recipe can be doubled.

"He who is greedy for gain troubles his own house; but he that hateth gifts shall live."

~Proverbs 15:27

Old Fashion Potato Salad

INGREDIENTS:

1 cup **mayonnaise**
3 tablespoons **white vinegar**
2 hard boiled **eggs**
3 lb. cooked **potatoes**
1 cup minced **onions**

1 teaspoon **salt**
1/4 teaspoon **pepper**
2 cups sliced **celery**

PROCEDURE:

1. In a large bowl, stir together mayonnaise, onions, vinegar, salt, pepper and eggs.
2. Peel and cube potatoes.
3. Add potatoes and celery to other ingredients, toss to coat well.
4. Cover and refrigerate for 4 hours.
5. If desired, sprinkle with paprika.

Make about 8 cups.

"Be careful for nothing; but in everything by prayer and supplication, with thanksgiving, let your requests be made known to God."
~Philippians 4:6

Pineapple Cole Slaw

INGREDIENTS:

4 cups shredded **cabbage**
1/2 cup **pineapple** tidbits (drained)
1/2 cup **seedless grapes** (cut in halves)
1/2 teaspoon **salt**
3/4 cup **salad dressing**

PROCEDURE:

1. Combine all ingredients.
2. Toss lightly.
3. Place in refrigerator for 30 minutes before serving.

"If a man is overtaken in any trespass, you who are spiritual restore such a one in a spirit of meekness; considering thyself, lest thou also be tempted."

~Galatians 6:1

Potato Salad

INGREDIENTS:

2 cups cooked diced **potatoes**
2 tablespoons chopped **pimento**
1 tablespoon chopped **green onion** tops
3 sliced hard boiled **eggs**
1/2 teaspoon **salt**

1/3 cup **mayonnaise**
1/3 cup **sour cream**

PROCEDURE:

1. Combine potatoes, pimento, onion tops, eggs and salt.
2. Mix mayonnaise and sour cream and add to potato mixture.
3. Toss lightly with a fork.
4. Chill and serve.

"O Magnify the lord with me, and let us exalt his name together."
~Psalm 34:3

Strawberry Salad

INGREDIENTS:

1 large pkg. strawberry **gelatin**
2 cups boiling **water**
2 10 oz pkgs. frozen **strawberries**
1 small can of crushed **pineapples**
3 **bananas**
1 cup **sour cream**

PROCEDURE:

1. Dissolved gelatin in boiling water.
2. Add strawberries and stir until thawed.
3. Add drained pineapple.
4. Add sliced bananas, mix well.
5. Pour 1/2 of mixture into mold and refrigerate until mold sets.
6. Leave balance of mixture at room temperature.
7. When mold is set, spread sour cream over top.
8. Pour remaining gelatin mixture over sour cream.
9. Refrigerate until ready to serve.

"I can do all things through Christ which strengtheneth me."
~Philippians 4:13

Barbecue Sauce For Beef

INGREDIENTS:

2 cups **ketchup**
2 cups **water**
1 clove **garlic**, finely chopped
1 tablespoon **chili powder**
2 tablespoons **Worcestershire sauce**

1 cup **sugar**
2 tablespoons **dry mustard**

PROCEDURE:

1. Mix all ingredients together.
2. Simmer slowly for 20 minutes.
3. Serve on Roast Beef.

Makes about 3 cups of sauce.

"Pray without ceasing."

~1 Thessalonians 5:17

Rough & Ready BBQ Sauce

INGREDIENTS:

2 medium **onions**, sliced
3/4 cup **ketchup**
3/4 cup **water**
2 tablespoons **vinegar**
2 tablespoons **Worcestershire sauce**
1 tablespoon **salt**

1/2 teaspoon **red pepper**
1 teaspoon **paprika**
1/2 teaspoon **black pepper**
1 teaspoon **chili powder**

PROCEDURE:

1. Combine all ingredients.
2. Heat and use as a sauce to baste meats or fish.

This sauce is especially good with lamb, pork or salmon. Makes 1-3/4 cups sauce.

NATHA'S TIP: You can do variations to this recipe as follows: For pork chops, use 1 cup condensed tomato soup instead of ketchup. Omit red pepper, add 1/8 teaspoon cinnamon, 1/8 teaspoon cloves and increase vinegar to 3 tablespoons.

"But godliness with contentment is great gain. For we brought nothing into this world and it is certain we can carry nothing out."
~I Timothy 6:6-7

Southern Barbecue Sauce

INGREDIENTS:

3 cups **ketchup**
1/2 cup **mustard**
2 cups **tomato sauce**
1 teaspoon **black pepper**
2 teaspoons **chili powder**
1 teaspoon **onion powder**
1 teaspoon **garlic powder**
1 teaspoon **salt**

PROCEDURE:

Mix all ingredients together and cook for 12 to 15 minutes, stirring constantly. Slowly add:

1/2 cup white sugar
1/2 cup brown sugar
1/4 cup vinegar
1/2 cup soy sauce
1/8 cup liquid smoke
1/8 cup Worcestershire sauce
1/2 teaspoon cayenne pepper

Cook slowly about 10 minutes more. Coat desired meat or fish, cook and enjoy.

NATHA'S TIP: For additional flavor add 1/4 teaspoon nutmeg.

"If any man be in Christ, he is a new creature. Old things are passed away and behold all things are become new."
~II Corinthians 5:17

Spicy Bar-B-Que Sauce

INGREDIENTS:

1 cup **ketchup**
1/2 cup **vinegar**
2 tablespoons **chili powder**
2 tablespoon **dry mustard**
6 tablespoon **brown sugar**

6 tablespoons **Worcestershire sauce**
1 teaspoon **margarine**

PROCEDURE:

1. Mix all ingredients together.
2. Boil for 5 minutes.
3. Then simmer until mixture thickens.
4. Serve on any meat of your choice.

Store unused portion in the refrigerator.

"Take therefore no thought for the morrow: for the morrow shall take thought for the things of itself. Sufficient unto the day is the evil thereof."

~Matthew 6:34

Tart Barbecue Sauce

INGREDIENTS:

1/2 cup **butter**
1 cup **vinegar**
1 **sour pickle**, finely chopped
2 tablespoons chopped **onion**
2 tablespoons **Worcestershire sauce**
2 tablespoons **chili sauce**

4 slices of **lemon**
1 teaspoon **brown sugar**
1 **green pepper,** finely chopped

PROCEDURE:

1. Combine all ingredients and mix thoroughly.
2. Place in a saucepan over low heat and cook until butter melts.
3. Stirring constantly.
4. Keep warm in a double boiler until ready to use on barbecued meats or as a sauce for barbecued sandwiches.

Makes 1-3/4 cups of sauce.

"Study to shew thyself approved unto God, a workman that needeth not to be ashamed, rightly dividing the word of truth."
~2 Timothy 2:15

Side Dishes

Baked Stuffed Potato

INGREDIENTS:

6 large **potatoes**
1 teaspoon **salt**
1 teaspoon minced **parsley**
2 tablespoon **butter or margarine**
2 tablespoon **milk**

PROCEDURE:

1. Place washed and scrubbed potatoes in oven and bake for 1 hour at 450 degrees.
2. Potatoes should be soft when pierced with knife.
3. Cut potatoes in halves lengthwise & scoop out cooked potato from skin.
4. Add salt, parsley, butter and milk and beat until light and fluffy.
5. Place this mixture gently back into potatoes skins.
6. Return to oven and brown for 5 to 8 minutes.

Makes 12 servings.

"But the manifestation of the Spirit is given to every man to profit withal."

~1 Corinthians 12:7

Bread Stuffing

INGREDIENTS:

3 cups **corn bread**
2 cups dry **bread**
1 teaspoon **salt**
1/8 teaspoon **black pepper**
1/4 teaspoon **poultry seasoning**
1/2 teaspoon finely chopped **onion**

1 teaspoon finely chopped **parsley**
2 tablespoons **butter**
1 **egg** (well beaten)
Giblet of fowl

PROCEDURE:

1. Soak bread in cold water, squeeze dry.
2. Season with salt, black pepper, poultry seasoning, parsley and onion.
3. Add melted butter and beaten egg.
4. Mix thoroughly.
5. Add giblet of fowl which has been chopped fine and boiled until nearly tender.

This stuffing will fill a three (3) to four (4) pound fowl.

"Now faith is the substance of things hoped for, the evidence of things not seen."

~Hebrews 11:1

Corn Bread Stuffing

INGREDIENTS:

2 cups **chicken broth**　　1 teaspoon **salt**
4 cups **cornbread**　　　　1 teaspoon **pepper**
1 medium **onion**
1 cup diced **celery**
2 **eggs** (beaten)
1/2 cup **butter**

PROCEDURE:

1. Break cornbread into small pieces.
2. Combine bread and chicken broth, mix to moisten bread
3. Add remaining ingredients, mix well.
4. Stuff into cavity of fowl and bake at 325 degrees until bird is done.

This is enough stuffing for a 4 pound duck or chicken.

"Humble yourselves in the sight of the Lord, and he shall lift you up."

~James 4:10

Potatoes In Sauce

INGREDIENTS:

1 tablespoon **butter or margarine**
1 medium sliced **onion**
1 teaspoon chopped **green pepper**
5 boiled **potatoes**
1 teaspoon **parsley**
1 teaspoon **salt**
1 teaspoon **black pepper**
1 cup of **gravy or thick broth**

PROCEDURE:

1. Melt butter in heavy sauce pan, sauté onion and green pepper (do not brown).
2. Slice potatoes in thick wedges and add to onion and green pepper.
3. Add parsley, salt pepper and gravy.
4. Cover and simmer until almost dry.

This dish should be watched closely so as not to burn. Makes 4 servings.

"O taste and see that the Lord is good: blessed is the man that trusteth in Him."

~Psalm 34:8

Sage Stuffing

INGREDIENTS:

3 cups soft **bread crumbs**
1/2 teaspoon **salt**
1/8 teaspoon **pepper**
1/3 cup **butter**
1 tablespoon minced **onion**
1 teaspoon **sage or poultry seasoning**

PROCEDURE:

1. Combine bread crumbs, sage, salt, pepper, butter and onion.
2. Toss lightly with a fork until blended.

This mixture will fill a four (4) pound fowl.

"As newborn babes, desire the sincere milk of the Word that ye may grow thereby."

~I Peter 2:2

Scalloped Potatoes

INGREDIENTS:

1/3 cup **margarine**
1/3 cup **flour**
2 cups **milk**
1 teaspoon **salt**
1/4 teaspoon **pepper**
8 oz sharp shredded **cheddar cheese**

2 tablespoon chopped **pimiento**
2 tablespoon minced **onions**
6 cups sliced cooked **potatoes**

PROCEDURE:

1. In a double boiler, combine margarine, milk, salt, flour and pepper.
2. Cook on low heat stirring constantly.
3. Add cheese and stir until cheese melts.
4. Add pimiento and onions.
5. Alternately place cooked potatoes and sauce in 1-1/2 quart greased casserole, begin with layer of potatoes and end with sauce on top.
6. Place in oven and bake at 350 degrees for 20 minutes.

Enjoy but don't hurt yourself.

"I am the way, the truth, and the life: no man cometh unto the Father, but by Me."

~John 14:6

Candied Sweet Potatoes

INGREDIENTS:

4 medium cooked or canned **sweet potatoes**
1/2 cup packed **brown sugar**
1/4 cup **butter or margarine**
1/2 cup **sugar**
1/4 cup **water**

PROCEDURE:

1. Cut potatoes in halves length wise and place in greased shallow baking dish.
2. Mix sugar, brown sugar, water and butter and bring to a boil.
3. Pour this mixture over potatoes.
4. Bake at 400 degrees for twenty minutes.
5. Baste potatoes several times with syrup in baking dish.

This makes an excellent side dish for almost any meal.

"O Lord our Lord, how excellent is thy name in all the earth! Who hast set thy glory above the heavens."

~Psalm 8:1

Christmas Punch

INGREDIENTS:

1 quart **pineapple juice**
1/4 pint **lemon juice**
2 cups **sugar**
2 cups boiling **water**
1 box **cherry gelatin**

PROCEDURE:

1. Dissolve gelatin in boiling water.
2. Add sugar, juices and enough water to make one gallon.
3. Serve with crushed ice.

"Love not the world, neither the things that are in the world. If any man love world, the love of the Father is not in him."

~I John 2:15

Fried Okra

INGREDIENTS:

2 cups sliced fresh **okra**
1/4 cup **corn meal**
1 teaspoon **season salt**
1/4 teaspoon **black pepper**
1/4 teaspoon **celery salt**
1/2 cup **salad oil**

PROCEDURE:

1. Trim ends of okra.
2. Cut into 1/4 inch slices.
3. Dredge in mixture of corn meal and seasonings.
4. Fry in hot oil until crisp and brown.
5. Drain on paper towel.

Note: Fresh okra can usually be found in your grocer's fresh vegetable section. If not available, try your local farmer's market.

"The Lord liveth; and blessed be my rock; and let the God of my salvation be exalted."

~Psalm 18:46

Fried Oysters

INGREDIENTS:

24 large **oysters**
2 **eggs**
1/2 teaspoon **salt**
1/8 teaspoon **pepper**
2 tablespoons cold **water**
1 cup bread **crumbs**

PROCEDURE:

1. Wash and drain oysters.
2. Beat eggs with seasonings, add water mix well.
3. Dip oysters into egg mixture, then into bread crumbs.
4. Let stand 5 minutes before frying.
5. Fry in hot oil until brown.

Serve at once.

"Lay not up for yourselves treasures upon earth, where moth and rust doth corrupt, and where thieves break through and steal: But lay up for yourselves treasures in heaven, where neither moth nor rust doth corrupt, and where thieves do not break through nor steal: For where your treasure is, there will your heart be also."
~Matthew 6:19-21

Hush Puppies

INGREDIENTS:

1 cup **corn meal**
2 teaspoons **baking powder**
1/2 teaspoon **salt**
1 small minced **onion**
1 **egg**

1 tablespoon **bacon grease or oil**
1/2 cup **milk**

PROCEDURE:

1. Sift all dry ingredients together.
2. Add onion and egg. Mix well.
3. Add oil and enough milk to make a stiff batter.
4. Form into little balls or patties.
5. Drop in deep hot oil and cook until golden brown.

Drain on paper towel and serve.

"A faithful man shall abound with blessings: but he that maketh haste to be rich shall not be innocent."

~Proverbs 28:20

Old Fashioned Lemonade

INGREDIENTS:

4 **lemons**
3/4 cup **sugar**
4 cups cold **water**

PROCEDURE:

1. Cut lemon in thin slices.
2. Remove seeds.
3. Place slices in bowl, add sugar.
4. Let stand for 10 minutes.
5. Press lemon slices with back of spoon to extract juice.
6. Add cold water.
7. Press lemon slices again.
8. Remove slices, strain mixture and serve over ice.

This is real lemonade.

"Whoso stoppeth his ears at the cry of the poor, he also shall cry himself, but shall not be heard."

~Proverbs 21:13

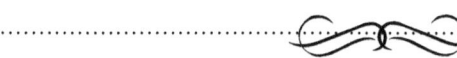

Pickled Beets

INGREDIENTS:

1/2 cup **vinegar**
2 tablespoons **sugar**
1/4 teaspoon **ground clove**
1/2 teaspoon salt 1 small **bay leaf**
1 small **onion**
1-15 oz can **beets** (sliced & cooked)

PROCEDURE:

1. Drain beets, save 1/4 cup of juice.
2. Mix beet juice, vinegar, sugar, salt, slices onion bay leaf and clove.
3. Bring this mixture to a boil.
4. Boil for five minutes.
5. Pour over beets and place in the refrigerator.

"The lips of truth shall be established for ever: but a lying tongue is but for a moment."

~Proverbs 12:19

Red Punch

INGREDIENTS:

1 package presweetened **cherry Kool-Aid**
1 package presweetened **strawberry Kool-Aid**
1 package presweetened **lemon Kool-Aid**
1 large can unsweetened **pineapple juice**
1 large bottle **Seven-up or Sprite**

PROCEDURE:

1. Place all ingredients in a gallon container.
2. Mix well.
3. Pour in enough water to fill container (mix again).
4. Mix again.
5. Pour into punch bowl.

"In thee, O Lord, do I put my trust: let me never be put to confusion?"

~Psalm 71:1

Southern Dumplings

INGREDIENTS:

2 cups sifted **flour**
2 teaspoons **baking powder**
1/2 cup **milk**
1 teaspoon **salt**
1/3 cup **shortening**
3 cups of **chicken stock**

PROCEDURE:

1. Sift flour, baking powder and salt together.
2. Cut in shortening mix with fork or blend with dough hooks.
3. Add enough milk to make stiff dough.
4. Roll out thin and cut into 1 inch squares.
5. Sprinkle lightly with flour and drop into boiling chicken stock.
6. Cover and boil gently for 30 to 40 minutes.

Options: Add boiled chicken parts or boiled chicken breast for additional flavor and texture.

"Blessed is the man that walketh not in the counsel of the ungodly, nor standeth in the way of sinners, nor sitteth in the seat of the scornful."

~Psalm 1:1

Vegetables

Mixed Greens

INGREDIENTS:

4 cups chopped rinsed **mustard greens or kale**
4 cups chopped rinsed **turnips**
2 teaspoons **black pepper**
1 teaspoon **salt**

PROCEDURE:

1. Place greens in a large pot of boiling water.
2. Cook greens rapidly (covered) on medium heat until tender, about twenty-five (25) minutes.
3. Season with salt and black pepper.
4. Serve with the liquid from the pot. (In the South this is called pot liquor)

NATHA'S TIP: For additional flavor with this dish, add salt pork, ham or smoked turkey to the boiling water; let simmer for 1 hour before cooking greens. After cooking, serve the selected meat along with the greens.

"Let everything that hath breath praise the Lord. Praise ye the Lord."

~Psalm 150:6

Southern Fried Corn

INGREDIENTS:

6 ears of **corn**
1/4 cup **bacon** dripping
2 tablespoons **flour**
1 cup **water**
1/4 cup **milk**
salt and pepper to your taste

PROCEDURE:

1. Clean corn and cut off the cob.
2. Add milk, water, salt, pepper and flour.
3. Fry in hot bacon dripping until done.

This is one southern dish that is sure to please.

NATHA'S TIP: If you cannot find corn on the cob, substitute three cans of whole kernel corn. The taste is not exactly the same but it is very close.

"I will bless the Lord at all times: His praise shall continually be in my mouth."

~Psalm 34:1

Southern Style Black-Eyed Peas

INGREDIENTS:

4 cups cooked **black eyed peas**
2 cups **water**
3/4 cup minced **onion**
1/2 cup chopped cooked **ham**
1/2 teaspoon **salt**
1/4 teaspoon **pepper**

PROCEDURE:

1. Combine all ingredients in a large saucepan.
2. Stirring well, bring to a boil over medium heat.
3. Reduce to low heat and simmer 20 to 25 minutes.
4. Stir often.

Note: Many people from the South could make a complete meal of this dish and some southern cornbread.

"I will call upon the Lord, who is worthy to be praised: so shall I be saved from mine enemies."

~Psalm 18:3

Bonus Recipe: Peach Cobbler

INGREDIENTS:

2 cans **peaches** (29 oz cans)
2 teaspoons **nutmeg**
2 teaspoons **cinnamon**
1/2 cup of **butter**

1 cup of **sugar**
Pie **crust** (two layers)

(For a larger pie you can double this recipe.)

PROCEDURE:

1. Cut peaches into small cubes.
2. Mix peaches, sugar, nutmeg, and cinnamon in a large bowl.
3. Melt butter and add to this mixture.
4. Place layer of pie crust in bottom of a 9" X 11" pan.
5. Pour peach mixture over this crust.
6. Add top crust.
7. Bake at 300 degrees for 1 1/2 hour or until crust is golden brown.

Note: Use Never Fail Pie Crust Recipe to make the crust for this cobbler.

"But God commendeth his love toward us, in that, while we were yet sinners, Christ died for us."

~Romans 5:8

More of Natha's Tips

COOKING WITH FRESH HERBS:

Moderation is the rule when cooking with herbs, fresh or dried. They should enhance the other flavors in the dish, never overwhelm them. More can always be added, but too much cannot be subtracted. When using dried herbs, crush the leaves in the palm of your hand before adding to the recipe. Herbs in leaf form, rather than powder, have fresher flavor. Get to know herbs by using them sparely in a recipe until you are familiar with their characteristics before you try blending several. When converting a favorite recipe that calls for dried herbs to fresh herbs, experiment first with the two times the amount given for dried before going to three.

Outlined below are some of the more popular herbs and suggestions for their use in various kinds of dishes.

Basil:

- Blend 1 tablespoon of chopped basil with 1/2 cup of butter to make a remarkable butter sauce for steak.
- Sprinkle 1 tablespoon chopped over pork chops after pan frying.
- Add a few slivers to lamb stew when adding vegetables.
- Baste roast chicken with Basil butter or add a few slivers to the cavity for extra flavor.

Marjoram:

- Add to braising liquids of pot roast and Swiss steaks.
- Rub one teaspoon chopped marjoram over pork shoulder or ham when roasting.
- Chop a few leaves and add to stuffing for chicken or turkey.
- Add to butter sauce for fresh vegetables. This will also add flavor to canned vegetables.

Oregano:
- To improve the taste of meatballs, add one teaspoon for each two pounds of meat.
- Sprinkle on cut up chicken. Bake with tomatoes.
- Add one tablespoon to spaghetti sauce or barbecue sauce.
- Add one teaspoon to tuna or salmon salad.
- Sprinkle on sliced cucumbers or tomatoes.

Rosemary:
- Sprinkle on hot coals when grilling beef.
- Sprinkle in hot oil when browning fried chicken.
- Heat canned peas, beans or corn with a few leaves. Drain and add butter.
- Especially good in chicken soup, homemade or canned. Add 1/2 teaspoon.

Sage:
- Add 1/2 teaspoon chopped leaves to chuck roast or meat loaf mixture.
- The favorite herb in old fashioned bread stuffing for turkey.
- Add 1/2 teaspoon in brown sauces for roast or in beef vegetable soups.
- Stir 1/2 teaspoon in macaroni and cheese before baking.

Tarragon:
- Add 1 teaspoon chopped leaves to simmering pot roast or corned beef.
- To saute ham, stir 1/2 teaspoon in pan gravy.
- Add 1 teaspoon to chicken casserole for an excellent flavor lifter.
- Add 1/2 teaspoon to scalloped potatoes, creamed potatoes or baked stuffed potatoes.
- Add 1/2 teaspoon to water when cooking macaroni or rice.

Thyme:

- Add chopped leaves to pork loin roast to fresh ham.
- Blend 1 teaspoon with 1/2 cup of butter or margarine when baking acorn squash.
- Crush several leaves in salad when making green salads.

SUBSTITUTING INGREDIENTS:

Cocoa For Chocolate:

Four tablespoons of cocoa plus 1/2 tablespoon Fat (butter or margarine) is equivalent to 1 ounce of chocolate.

Powdered Eggs For Whole Eggs:

Two tablespoons of powdered eggs plus 2-1/2 tablespoons of water is equivalent to 1 whole egg.

Regular Flour For Self Rising Flour:

One cup of all-purpose flour plus 1-1/2 teaspoons baking powder and 1/2 teaspoon salt is equivalent to one cup of self rising flour for recipes purposes.

Index

Angel Biscuits	12
Angel Corn Sticks	13
Baked Stuffed Potatoes	84
Baking Powder Biscuits	14
Barbecue Sauce For Beef	76
Barbecued Baby Back Ribs	52
Beef Stew From Scratch	53
Big Pound Cake	26
Bonus Recipe: Peach Cobbler	107
Bread Stuffing	85
Butter Pound Cake	27
Buttermilk Fried Chicken	54
Buttermilk Pound Cake	28
Buttermilk Tea Cakes	29
Can't Fail Rolls	15
Candied Sweet Potatoes	92
Chicken And Dumplings	55
Chicken Gumbo	56
Chicken Salad	66
Chicken With Vegetables	57
Chili For The Crowd	58
Christmas Punch	93
Coconut-Pecan Filling &Frosting	30
Cole Slaw With Color	67
Corn Bread Stuffing	86
Deviled Eggs	46
Deviled Eggs With Pimiento	47
English Pea Salad	68

Fried Okra	94
Fried Oysters	95
German Chocolate Cake	31
German Style Beef Stew	59
Glorified Baked Beans	60
Good Pound Cake	32
Good Sugar Cookies	33
Hush Puppies	96
Macaroni Salad	69
Mixed Greens	104
Natha's Dinner Rolls	16
Natha's Favorite Pie Crust	34
Never Fail Pie Crust	35
Old Fashioned Apple Pie	36
Old Fashioned Lemonade	97
Old Fashioned Lemon Pie	37
Old Fashioned Potato Salad	70
Pancakes From Scratch	17
Pickle Beets	98
Picnic Eggs	48
Pineapple Coleslaw	71
Potato Salad	72
Potatoes And Ham	61
Potatoes In Sauce	87
Quick Buttermilk Biscuits	18
Quick Muffins	19
Red Punch	99
Rough & Ready Barbecue Sauce	77
Sage Stuffing	88

Scalloped Potatoes	89
Scrambled Eggs	49
Scratch Cornbread	20
Seven Up Pound Cake	38
Southern Barbecue Sauce	78
Southern Corn Bread (#1)	21
Southern Corn Bread (#2)	22
Southern Dumplings	100
Southern Fried Corn	105
Southern Style Black Eyed Peas	106
Spicy Bar-B-Que Sauce	79
Strawberry Salad	73
Swedish Tea Cakes	39
Sweet Potato Pie (#1)	40
Sweet Potato Pie (#2)	41
Tart Barbecue Sauce	80
Tea Cakes	42
Turkey Hash	62
Two Egg Layer Cake	43

Notes:

www.ingramcontent.com/pod-product-compliance
Lightning Source LLC
Chambersburg PA
CBHW071712040426
42446CB00011B/2033